For Yukie and Haruo Kimura —K. K.

Special thanks to Takayuki Kondō, Masahiro Asano, Kunio Kirisawa, Masaharu Yamamoto, Maiko Ōsakaya, Miya Eda, Kotori Eda, Chikara Kimura, Uta Kimura, Rachel Sheinkin, David Sheinkin, and the late Yasue Tenmei, for the use of her memoir.

. . .

Published by Roaring Brook Press
Roaring Brook Press is a division of Holtzbrinck Publishing Holdings Limited Partnership
120 Broadway, New York, NY 10271 • mackids.com

Our books may be purchased in bulk for promotional, educational, or business use.
Please contact your local bookseller or the Macmillan Corporate and Premium Sales Department
at (800) 221-7945 ext. 5442 or by email at MacmillanSpecialMarkets@macmillan.com.

Library of Congress Cataloging-in-Publication Data is available.
First edition, 2023

The art for this book was rendered using oil on canvas and adjustments in Photoshop.
The typefaces are ArenaNewBQ and PT Serif. The book was edited by Connie Hsu, and designed
and art directed by Jen Keenan. The production was managed by Allene Cassagnol,
and the production editor was Kathy Wielgosz.

Printed in China by RR Donnelley Asia Printing Solutions Ltd.,
Dongguan City, Guangdong Province

ISBN 978-1-250-20650-3
1 3 5 7 9 10 8 6 4 2

YUKIE'S ISLAND

My Family's World War II Story

written by **Yukie Kimura,**
Kōdo Kimura,
and **Steve Sheinkin**

illustrated by
Kōdo Kimura

Roaring Brook Press
New York

When I was eight years old, my family
lived alone on a tiny island with a lighthouse.

I knew my country was at war.
But the fighting felt far away.

My father was the lighthouse keeper,
and I was his helper.

Until my brother, Yoshio, yelled,
"Yukie, come on!"

Then we were off on a new day of adventures.

We were explorers

and scientists.

You had to be brave to get seagull eggs.
But we needed them to make cookies.

We were treasure hunters.
And secret keepers.

Except our sister, Yasue,
who preferred to read.

We were sailors too, a crew of three on the high seas.
It was the only way to get to school.

One morning, my lunch box fell overboard.
The fish had a party that day.

When I looked up from the water,
I forgot all about my lunch.

The fighting wasn't far away anymore.

"Do *not* talk about the war in town," Yasue told us. "You can be punished for saying we are losing."

I didn't know things were going so badly.

We still went to school for the next few weeks.

But it wasn't the same.

"It will all be over soon,"
my father said.

Time is slow when
you're waiting.

Even for
something bad.

At night, my father
played his bamboo flute.

The music sounded like
things he was afraid to say.

The American planes came on a Saturday.
And again on Sunday. We were all at home.

We got to the shelter before the bombs started falling.

The scream of the engines and explosions
went on
and on.

The war ended soon after that.

But not everyone
came back to school.

It was a cold winter.
I helped my mother make hats and
sweaters from green army blankets.
My father played his flute at night.

The music sounded
like things I wished
I didn't know.

From the top of the lighthouse,
I watched the sky.

"There's nothing to be scared
of now," my father said.

I was not so sure.

And one day,

I saw something . . .

There were shapes in the fog,
moving on the water.

"Yukie, come on!" Yoshio shouted
as he ran toward the shore.

"Our teacher told us about this," Yasue
said. "It's the ice floes from Russia!"

Yoshio jumped on.

It sounded like the seals were laughing at him.

I was scared. I waited.

Then I jumped.

We were explorers

and scientists, with very cold feet.

Soon the sun began to set.
But no one wanted to go inside.

A NOTE FROM STEVE

Yukie Kimura (born Yukie Suzuki) was born in 1937, the youngest of three siblings. Yukie's father, Shigeyoshi, worked as a lighthouse keeper in Hokkaidō, northern Japan, and when Yukie was six years old, the family moved to Bentenjima, an island a few hundred yards off the coast of the small city of Nemuro. Yukie's earliest memories are of being plunked down in a wonderland. Yukie's father maintained the island's two lighthouses, and the family of five—including Yukie's mother, Tomie; sister, Yasue; and brother, Yoshio—lived in the only house on the island.

This photo was taken around 1942, at the studio in Kushiro, Hokkaidō, when Yukie was five years old. (From left: Yasue, Shigeyoshi, Yoshio, Yukie, and Tomie.)

It seems like an idyllic life for an intrepid kid, and Yukie describes it that way, but consider the time line: The family moved to the island in 1943, in the middle of World War II. By 1945, when Yukie was eight, Allied forces were closing in on Japan, bombing city after city. No corner of the country was safe, not even a remote town on the northeastern edge of Hokkaidō.

Fast-forward seventy-two years, to the suburbs of New York City on a night in late 2017. I was talking with Kōdo, my sister Rachel's longtime partner, who happens to be a painter, and he started telling stories about his mother, a woman named Yukie who'd grown up on a tiny island in Japan during World War II. Images formed in the air as he spoke: the lighthouses and the sea, Yukie and her brother collecting seagull eggs and digging for treasure in caves, their mother in her garden, their father playing his flute at night.

It was a picture book. It had to be a picture book!

We agreed from the start that this would be a true story, Yukie's story, based directly on her memories, along with our own research of the setting and historical events of those years. Yukie still lives in Hokkaidō and, with Kōdo as translator between English and Japanese, I was able to ask her lots of questions. She made beautiful sketches of the island, showing the layout of its buildings and other features, and these were essential references for both the written story and the art.

Of course, after seventy-plus years, she could not possibly recall exactly when certain things happened—dropping her lunch in the ocean, for instance, or finding artifacts in the cave. We took some liberties arranging these memories into a narrative and condensing the action into one year. Yukie encouraged us to do this—to take her stories and, in her words, "play." And that word— *play*—was very important to us while making this book. Even given the frightening aspects of her story, Yukie recalls her childhood as happy, thrilling—"a really great and special memory."

A NOTE FROM KŌDO

Bentenjima is very close to the city of Nemuro in Hokkaidō, Japan, but to my mother it felt far away. Strong winds and high tides often made it impossible for small boats to get to or from the island. For Yukie, this made her home feel like its own little world.

Life on the island was very basic. There was no electricity—the lighthouse lights used acetylene gas. Evenings were lit by oil lamps or candlelight. They carried water from a well and collected rainwater in a barrel. My mother and her family grew vegetables, caught fish, and gathered clams, scallops, sea urchins, kelp, and seaweed. When the family's chickens weren't laying enough eggs, Yukie and her brother, Yoshio, hunted for seagull eggs. My grandfather even used traditional methods to make his own sea salt.

Yukie and Yoshio loved to dig in caves, though they did not know much about the treasures they found. In fact, the soil of Bentenjima is full of fragments of earthenware, stone arrowheads, and tools dating back over 1,500 years. Today, the whole island is designated an ancient archaeological site.

My mother and I are standing at the port of Nemuro on November 15, 2018, with Bentenjima Island behind us. Even though the sky was clear, the local fisherman told us the sea was too rough that day for the small boat to take me to the island. Fortunately, I was able to go the next day.

Yukie's sister, Yasue, spent most of her time reading and studying, which is why she's always shown with a book. My grandparents were very proud of her, and my mother says it was obvious to everyone how smart her older sister was. Yasue went on to become a schoolteacher.

During the school year, my grandfather rowed Yukie and her siblings to the mainland for school. Sometimes Yasue would help row. While it was an adventure for the children, it wasn't always easy. Whenever there was a high tide, even on nice days, the children had to stay on the island. Or they might be stuck in town after school, and would have to stay at a family friend's house.

The ship that Yukie saw from the boat wasn't a military ship. By the summer of 1945, the Japanese navy had run low on battleships and cargo ships. Most had been sent to the South Pacific. The ships near Bentenjima were chartered by the navy from private companies—even fishing companies. Many of these were sunk by American submarines.

My grandfather played his bamboo flute, called a shakuhachi, throughout his life. It was one of his few hobbies, as maintaining the lighthouses kept him busy from early morning to late at night. It always sounded to me like wind, something from nature. A

We visited the air raid memorial at Narumi Park in Nemuro.

meditative and lonely sound. He tried to teach me when I was young (he passed away in 1986). It was difficult to make a nice sound.

The American air raid on Nemuro and Bentenjima spanned two days, starting early in the morning on July 15, 1945, with the most devastating attack on the second day. My mother and her family were in their air raid shelter for about eleven hours that day. My mother tells me it felt even longer because it was so frightening. Bombs and the fires they caused destroyed 80 percent of Nemuro, burning 2,300 houses and killing around 400 people.

The war ended on August 15, 1945, one month after the attack. In the image of Yukie in her classroom, I painted American military outside the window. They visited the school to make sure no one was teaching the children militarism and far-right nationalistic philosophy.

The last paintings in the book show Yukie and her siblings playing on ice floes that naturally floated south from Russia, which is close to Bentenjima in northern Japan. It is actually very dangerous to play on an ice floe. This is why my grandparents look so unhappy in this scene. If you fall into the icy water, you could die within minutes. You could also fall in between the floes and get stuck underwater. Today, this is officially prohibited by the government. You can walk on the ice only with a trained tour guide while wearing a special wetsuit.

Throughout the book, I have included small pink flowers in many of the scenes. The flower is called Hamanasu (Ramanas rose). My mother said this rose symbolized her childhood memories, which are sweet like the jam you can make from the rose hip.

I used many references to illustrate this book: my mother's stories and journals; information from books, authorities, memoirs, and interviews; and hundreds of photographs. For details of the bombing, my main source was *Nemuro Air Raid*, compiled by the Nemuro Air Raid research group. They interviewed survivors and included research from the local Nemuro government and US military archives. I also spoke to key members of this research group directly, including Mr. Takayuki Kondō, (eighty-eight years old at the time) who was an eyewitness to the air raid.

I grew up in the city of Hakodate, in southern Hokkaidō, but had never seen the place where my mother spent her childhood. In 2018, about seventy-five years after my family left the island, I visited Bentenjima. The island is now overgrown with grass, and it's hard to see where the house and the lighthouse that was destroyed once stood. But the white lighthouse stands strong and is still in use, though it is automated now. My mother joined me in Nemuro on that trip, where we paid respects at the stone memorial carved with the names of the air raid's 354 identified and 39 unidentified victims.

I'd like this story to commemorate the ordinary citizens and families who were killed or hurt by these air raids. It seems so senseless, with the war ending a month later. In total, the air raids during those two days in Hokkaidō took more than two thousand lives. Estimates of total Japanese civilian deaths caused by US air raids during World War II range from 200,000 to 400,000.

In *Yukie's Island*, I wanted to show the real people who lived through this time. Survivors are affected by war. I'd heard stories about my mother and her family since I was small. They're so familiar that I feel like I experienced them myself. Even so, since this is my first picture book, it took me a while to figure out how to approach creating a story with people I know. I slowly found a way for me to see it, like creating a movie. When I thought about each scene, my mind started traveling to Bentenjima as my pen and brush followed. I started feeling the light, sound, air, winds—almost experiencing the scene as one of the family members. If you can feel even a little bit of that, I would be very happy.

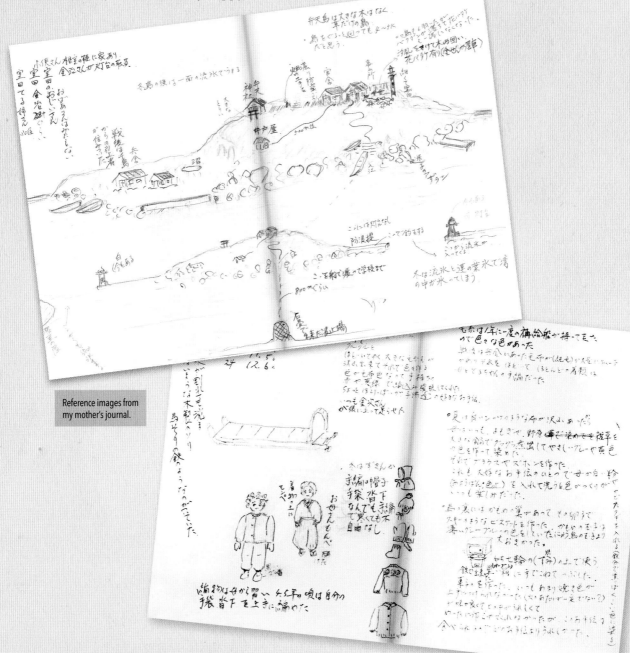

Reference images from my mother's journal.